Straya

Straya
paul summers

Smokestack Books
1 Lake Terrace, Grewelthorpe, Ripon HG4 3BU
e-mail: info@smokestack-books.co.uk
www.smokestack-books.co.uk

Text copyright 2017,
Paul Summers, all rights reserved.

ISBN 978-0-9955635-1-3

Smokestack Books is
represented by Inpress Ltd

*for ash, ryan & aaron
& in memory of mam.*

Contents

straya
obligato	13
building eden	14
allegorical	15
malbooma	16
cyclone	18
the man who mourned trees	19
march fly sonata	20
leichardt saw the light	21
the rainbow	22
big picture	23
at black gin leap	24
the rivermen	26
fish out of water	27
the life of clouds	28
the republic of crows	29
votive	30
revision	32
pastoral 1	33
pastoral 2	34
fugue	35
drouth	36
prophecy	37
one hundred head of cattle	38
the birds	39
rope trick	40
cane toad blues	41
8 count	42
dark music	43
on days like these	44
pool	45
curriculum	46
the lucky country	47
pout	49
feral	50

reading carl rogers	51
petrichor 1	52
petrichor 2	53
palimpsest	54
terra australis	55
victory waltz	56
epistle to a great-nephew	57
mappa mundi	59
a preface to the fall	60
threnody	61
the watchers	62
song of remiel	63
les souixante-huitards	64
fan ho's vehement lens	66
the shortest day	69
exit	70
dear john	71

guerra

carmina mortuorum	81
legion	86
fighting fifth	87
bait	88
plantation road	89
flowers of evil	90
i.m. ibrahim dawawsa	91
gaza july 2014	92
yukurru	93
textbook execution	94
ptsd	95

cadenza
cadenza	99
the aftermath	113
flare	120
ferryman	121
life lessons from the mermaid cafe	122
paradise by the dashboard light	123
fall	124
i wish for him this	125
cv	126
crucible	127
archaeology	128
grieve	130

Acknowledgements 131

straya

obligato

the movement begins
grave but consolatory

storm-bird & curlew
& breath percussive

histories & latency
indentured by dread

the contract of guilt
disavowal's blunt rider

& the dirt will sing
each phrase redemptive

spilled blood made concrete
by the pressure of hours

recast in memoriam
into fists of dense ochre

building eden / pathology

first, transport a destitute & 'criminalised' underclass to a largely inhospitable territory. police/domineer/subjugate them with a militarised administration of god-fearing, self-serving, conservative, imperialist keepers. let them loose with a slightly dysfunctional model of self-betterment & proto-capitalism. promote aspiration & deference in equal measure. grasp the idyll of painless heather. dream of the stag & the snow draped weasel. feign classlessness whilst remaining subordinate to monarchy & the church. exact genocide. deny consequence. never bother to learn how to spell egalitarianism. cultivate the anxieties of an insecurely attached child plagued by catholic guilt. mistrust all thought & reflection but celebrate athleticism, larrikinism & anything remotely automotive. actively encourage the adoption of the outmoded & morally irreprehensible ideologies of white-supremacism, patriarchy & homophobia. allow countless profiteering global corporations to rape the land of its finite resources. at all costs do not properly tax or regulate them. exempt yourself from any complicity in the doomsday scenarios of global warming. she'll be right. sign up to a gestural federal model of governance but continue to behave like the six anachronistic & protectionist colonies you have always been. embrace america, with all her malls & homogenous car-parks, her prematurely sexualised child performers, her gun laws & her pretty dreams. embrace china. she's loaded. hate cane toads & asylum seekers with equal vigour. employ the hollow concepts of *mateship*, *a fair go* & *a light upon the hill* ad nauseam in any rhetorical context, appropriate or not, when in the cold light of june they mean fuck all. issue a raft of muttered half-meant apologies that are & will remain for the foreseeable just words. choke on the lines of a scotsman's florid anthem. stick your pension on a nag, cremate another tasteless snag, crack open a cold stubby to wash it all away.

allegorical

daybreak plays out
frisking on the skin
of a silent lake
a pale autistic boy
is lost in the bush

all fear constrained
he revels as a ripple
unravels on the bank
a language of muteness
communing with season

he squats oblivious
beneath the gums
his eyes aversive
to the gape of salvation

malbooma

cyclone marcia, 2015

grievous as the scour
of a cello's loosened strings

the vehemency of threnody
announces the approach.

skewered on a shard
of her furious breath

the scent of petrichor
& fractured gum, the prick

of an ocean's pillaged salt,
the ferric lick of static.

& crudely stitched in indian file,
a hundred head of hunch-back

steers have taken their leave;
sought shelter in the hollow

of the billabong's nadir.
the birds are grounded,

the insects too, their thatch
of song drowned out or muted.

one fierce whip
of her raging tongue

sees spastic foliage
shredded to a pulp;

its morning gloss reduced
to drifts of powdered jade.

contorted boughs capitulate,
their lumbering age undone.

& wrapped around the straining girth
of whitey's paddock's sturdiest tree,

a clump of opaque kangaroos
commit themselves to parliaments

of dread & doubt, bipartisan & silent,
resign themselves to fragile fate;

to marcia's prerogative of callous indifference,
the pang of malbooma's recalcitrant wrath.

cyclone

contrary to the advice
of the disaster management
communiqué, i re-read conrad's
typhoon as my principal preparation;
muster the essentials: a golden cache
of tobacco & rum, a sack of plump
pistachios, capacity for light & sound,
my nearest & my dearest.

we huddle in the gloom
of the laundry's bland cell;
stripped down to the bloom
of anxious skin, like the crewmen
of *das boot,* pending the percussion
of depth-charge or mine.

the man who mourned trees

loose rings release
their frantic souls

integrity dissolved
to feathered ash

the dirt absorbing
their hard-won age

months since the storm
& still it burns; red-raw,

the muted pyre
of fallen trees

amber sap-scent
on the breeze

a quiet bulge
of beryl smoke

evolves by turns
from frozen speech

to ghost stampede
then taking stock

or paused for breath
it squats like grief

in the hollows
of the wetlands

march fly sonata

obdurate as doubt
they plague the day;

corralling us in cycles
of reconnaissance & strike.

the drone of passage,
the heat of execution,

a blood-lust to puncture
our softened hides.

short-lived in the bell-jar
of this capricornian heat,

un-haunted by histories,
a conscience unfranked.

as guiltless as vampires
they colonise the plain.

leichardt saw the light

we chase the curves
the min min's glow

seduced by her dance
of curious prospect

the bulge of the possible
the joy of not knowing

these charts are bankrupt
all precept defaulted

each contour blank
& freed of enclosure

the arc of the liminal
melting into black

all our scant narratives
drawn to their conclusion

the rainbow

still loyal to hope
despite betrayals

we chase its tail
through pitiful skies

hewed from the lips
of their last anoxic kiss

our lungs igniting
the chinaman's paddock

not gilded crocks
but ossuaries

the hollow bones
of love & hate

their quiet journey
to realms of dust

big picture

like tarnished gelt,
the light in free-fall,

trips on the lips
of a petulant wave;

the gulls interpreting
each blank inflexion.

beyond this moment,
beyond its calm,

a hunger stalks
the stoic poor.

losses compiled
& grief observed.

the clerics bleat
at the altar of betrayal.

a slow march to exile
for our constituted souls.

& the bees are oblivious,
each threnody unheard,

all empathy imprisoned
in the matrix of their gossip.

they swoon in the syrup
of the season's lush feast,

draining off the nectar
from each profligate bloom.

at black gin leap

beyond the brink
only the fall

a plump confederacy
of chalk-faced angels

gathers on a ledge
the edge of schism

red dirt solipsists
rocking on their heels

reflecting on the torment
of their freckled pasts

a shit-face cocktail
of opposites:

of travesty & idyll
of fetid hulks

& oil-paint stags
of servitude

& eureka's cloth stars
of shark-eyed monarchs

& martyred thieves
of calvin & the papal bull

of flame & flood
of parch-mouthed drought

of rape, of love
of murder, of shame

of histories severed
& gallipoli's gaunt legion,

of guilt, of joy,
of fear, of hope

advance australia fair

beyond the brink
only the fall

savour the coldness
of the onrushing air.

the river-men

rockhampton, qld.

all history blurs
toonooba slurs

her sacred song
induced to trance

her skin a throng
of dervish loons

a maelstrom dance
of fractured moons

the river-men
reclaim the shore

each toke, each mis-told
joke invokes a roar

the river-men
reduced to shapes

the twilight drapes
in analgesic fog

the petrichor
of smoke & grog

their catch un-bagged
their song-lines snagged

on the burr of their throats
they dream themselves

they dream themselves
invincible in dingo-tail coats

fish out of water

unlikely in its grace
the stingray airborne

jettisons all thoughts
of lumpen weight

an idling flap
a sideways glance

the gloss of its wings
relishing the air

the whip of its tail
cracking in the blue

we sideline our awe
in favour of motive

the trajectory of survival
the arc of possibility

the life of clouds

anointed by maternal sun
the muted thermals preen,
prostrated in their undertow,
they lick her tattered edges clean.
birth-cries stifled in the blur of space,
your quickening lungs a rolling boil;
giddy on the thinness of flawless air.

swoon, you glorious, tumbling child,
melt into the brilliance of your lovers'
dense arms. learn rapture in a lawless
spume. transience in shadow. the slow
dance of witness. the knowing glance
of stuttering time. every breathing
minute confronted by its ending.

the republic of crows

each punctuated eye
a lifeless bead, ownerless
as void estates whose forfeit
deeds have rotted into porridge;

their gathering is murderous,
devoid of grief, without remorse,
their spite in chorus & refrain
insatiable the crows grow hoarse.

the dutchman's gift, this colony
of bird; where scant confession
goes unheard, where soil is cursed
& absolution borne in silence.

votive

sedate the day she died,
the sea as nonchalant
as one avowed to tide
can be, left maudlin slack
& to her own devices.
& somewhere south
a fire is raging,
burn-off or pyre,
its feral flames conspire
to daub the liminal
with slicks of cold chert.
a cormorant bears
his jet-black cross,
the tern will measure
each fatal swoop,
a trawler plods
its net corpse heavy.
& clouds keep time,
each hour compiled
in blank compendia.
the fish do not bite.
my bait sun-cooked
& stale like grand
ideas denied fruition,
like sweetmeat love
left festering for want
of voice or fear of failure,
like palm-warmed gelt
un-spendable on foreign
days. i tie a running hitch
to snare some memory
or a smile, a rein to halt
the pull of keening;
not fit for purpose
my knot unravels,

each unkempt end
reluctant to be joined.
the breeze expounds
her lisping votive
& clouds keep time,
their callous task
unrushed, each careful
hour polished & re-polished
'til fashioned to a finish.

revision

the man from snowy river
takes a well-earned break

freed from the monotony
of the romantic aussie icon

he kicks off his boots
throws down his hat

scrubs off the reek
of lathered horse

he paws through the pages
of his mother's hefty bible

pours a cool beer
has a quick wank

imagining the black girls
they'd raped at tulloch ard

pastoral

the wind lacks focus
it plaits the fronds
of servile palms

incites their tongues
to dog-eared hymns
& rote learned psalms

gaunt faces gaze
redrawn in rust
on slumping roofs

they dance a waltz
funereal & kept to time
by stuttering hooves

the paddock recanting
its heritage of dust

pastoral 2

the land, in fever,
spits out a knot

of holy tongues
at feral goats

& scrawny steers.
they cross themselves,

then drop prostrate
in wafts of dust.

& here, in the glow
of indentured light;

the lucky perfect
exquisite spite,

the insular men,
their hatred of the other.

fugue

drought-kissed the grasses
melt; a voile of dust & stubborn
seed which eddies lift to lay as
shroudson lumpen cairns of bone
& hide. only the hymn of solemn
fly, of rattle-boned locust, of fragile
breath. a trinity indentured to earth
in fever. the ghost gum dreams
the dam-ponds full, the highlands
flaunting their green ascents,
storm-cloud whipped to stiffened
peaks; & up on high, your callous god,
his beard of flame, his frozen eyes,
astride the basalt's jagged flight.

drouth

dago-built, the silos wilt
each acre mortgaged to the hilt

each unlit pyre of hide & bones
like barren seed amongst the stones

the dam-ponds drained
the bleat of prayers refrained

cloth-eared, a season's blunt incursion
ignoring each amended version

to go about its thrifty toil
to break a marriage with the soil

the reek of petrichor drifts west
delivered like some callous jest

a wicked ruse at god's behest
the fledgling cuckoo in the nest

prophecy

the cotton drifts along the road
escapes a semi-trailer's load

a tractor tills a thirsty field
a dust-cloud prophecy of yield

a brumby tends its bow-legged foal
the downs trepanned prospecting coal

the ledger casts them cap-in-hand,
their progeny forfeits the land

like moths they make their frenzied flight
drawn by the aura of city light

& here, where heritage becomes its ghost
each rain-drop savoured like the host

like fumbled first kisses, like youth undone
they hold it on their tongues until it is gone.

one hundred head of cattle walking to their slaughter

gaunt brahman plod,
driven by thirst
or herdsman's prod,
they taunt the day
to do its worst.

the judas steer
sticks to his course;
a black pearl tear
betraying remorse.
he dreams all time

unwound, his guilt
absolved. in such
slow lines as these
all history resolved.

the birds

& johnno hates
the cockatoos

fearing the gist
of jet-black news

his auntie's lore
the bleak rapport

between the birds
& sheol's hoar

a death forewarned
a loss un-mourned

a fatal tumour
an hideous rumour

a prophecy encrypted
in the sheen of their plumes

rope-trick

flanked by two
complicit trees

a sepia clot
of bulging smoke

grows upwards
like a faqir's rope.

drought-licked,
the paddock strains

to raise a smile;
its colour drained,

the future harboured
in its roots.

we hanker for the thrill
of a side-kick's ascent.

cane toad blues

a cane-toad sings the blues
a belching confessional
of lonesome self-loathing

of existential torment
his unrequited verses
hanging from a bridge

& the mozzies play jazz,
choking on the high-notes
of their own importance

their blood-soaked horns
lamenting the confinement
of every bitter form

this air an anthem
for the misunderstood

8 count

& casual, almost,
he lands his punch.

precision maintained
through a flailing arc.

a drumlin ridge of knuckles
colliding with her orbit.

bloodless, for a moment,
the lesion gapes, its edges

fashioned to a pout.
her body percussive

as it hits the floor;
drum-hollow but dense,

like sides of meat slapped
down on butchers' blocks.

dark music

within each slap
of lawless wind
the straining vowels
of rebel songs
grown old & lame

within each wave
the ocean spits
her bilious rage
each breaker tipped
with blunt indictment

within each flume
of sepia smoke
the trees lament
their dead set free
their souls to rest

within the gloss
of petrol eyes
& palsied smiles
the weight of loss
the soil's dark music

on days like these

when light flirts
melting the beat
of northern soul

a koel is mourning
the passing of clouds
history grows slowly

we marvel at snails
the pace of leaves
a breeze reconciled

we load our bags
with difficult things
walk nowhere fast

our ankles manacled
to the deadweight of sun

pool

consumed in a dance
of turquoise & sun

their ecstasy escapes
the nonsense of play

the foaming flumes
of belly-flop & bomb

their laughter locked
in transient bubbles

oblivious to audience
my sons transformed

as lithe & naked
as blissful fish

honorary professors
in the school of joy

curriculum

they are learning to read;
the lexicon of rod & line,

the breath of tide, the kiss
of breeze, of bream knock

& crab, the cadence of weed,
the cautious enquiries

of thumb-print perch,
the heft of a ray's reluctant

wings, set anchored & corpse-
heavy, the slalom run of a loom-

shuttle shark, the lazy cod,
the tarpon's slick violence,

the thrill of the strike,
the sanctity of losses.

the lucky country

like swallows we will leave
when the sun glows cold

the coral blooms
its slick of martial red

commemorates
the pointless dead

of oyster cove
of dardanelles

of helmand's dirt
of watch-house cells

each morgue replete
with innocents

*

& see them smile
the lucky ones

each prosperous
yet bankrupt

their sun-dried lips
set fast & thin

in lavish pouts
in larrikin grins

their guilt grown bloated
on exuberant spite

*

& hear them sing
the lucky ones

a murderous choir
of wagging tongues

each consonant
& vowel hamstrung

consenting to silence
no questions asked

each verse does violence
each chorus the denial

*

the tern will measure
each fatal swoop

the hangmen hitch
each deadly loop

the battered wife
renews her vows

the learned entrench
in furrowed brows

each idyll is undone
at the hands of truth

pout

a complicated light;
the sort of night

when edward hopper
would have painted you

reading by storm lamp
in a foxed veranda glow.

(had he ever lived adjacent
& been no longer extinct.)

as neither is so, i marvel
in this slowest dusk

at flawless lines of neck
& arm, the swell of hip,

your silent lips awaiting
the burden of a hero's kiss.

feral

our dead are graved
the children put to bed

cold moonlight daubed
on blue-lipped roofs

this wine is blood
this wine is ink

language grown knotted
in the chaos of its spells

we stumble over logic
wrestle with our truths

& distant lightning
mimes a storm

a blade to the heart
of this feral night

reading carl rogers on the beach at yeppoon

the ocean holds
a mirror to the land

flagging the poles
of its pendulous moods

inertia & hostility
blank denial & strenuous guilt

the larrikin & the mute
the virgin & the whore

but always the fear
roughly embroidered

on its callous heart
like monograms

on handkerchiefs
their grandpas cherished

petrichor 1

a sudden gush
of summer rain

a dart for cover
laughter drowned

a canopy of elder
a fate demanded

four eager hands
an awkward fly

a gloss of sweat
the cool of skin

our violent lips
our fingers delve

a kind of silence
the smell of wet

petrichor 2

the season slides
towards a close

no beat no cadence
to guide our dance

& after the storm
not petrichor

not sweetness
or cherished calm

only the reek
of thin-lipped spite

grown overripe
& festering

beneath the fierceness
of this sun

palimpsest

i.m. arthur stace

five slabs east
of the druggist

on pitt street
one gaunt word

in copperplate
fragile as dawn

clinging like lichen
to sweating stone

neither statement
nor prayer

arthur's cruel god
flirting with irony

all our eternities
permanent as chalk

terra australis

burdened again
by the weight of light

the she-oaks stoop
in hunched indifference.

bored with transit
the waves collapse

hissing disapproval
at undesired landfall.

a raft of red-faced soil
complicit in its silence.

& opal-eyed, a threnody
of jigging crows forewarn

of loss; gloat over details
of another sunken boat.

victory waltz

the vanquished watch
the victors dance

gag on the cloy
of their painted smiles

marvel at the straightness
of their calvinist spines

each stilted step
joyless & by rote,

reined in by precept
(by gene or meme)

their thin-lipped mouths
re-canting a three-count

their pretty frocks
hemmed with dysfunction

epistle to a great-nephew

pin your heart onto your sleeve
show tenderness to those who grieve

look kindly on the tramp in rags
parade your hope like battle-flags

rejoice in the heave of a songbird's chest
& never let your dreams find rest

learn the lexicon of grace
that beauty lives in every face

do not fear silence, or the night
defend the truth, resist all spite

embrace the things you do not know
hear music in the silent snow

find art in the lines of someone's hips
in perfect goals & home-cooked chips

be strong, be frail
be bold enough to fail

& even in the darkest days
make time to smile, to offer praise

cherish the perfume of summer rain
let passion dance through every vein

do not be bought or swayed by fashion
declaim injustice, perfect compassion

treasure the living, honour the dead
let swallows fly within your head

tailor your promises to your means
never bow to kings or queens

fill your soul with laughter's hymn
master your pride & learn to swim

but most of all, amidst life's thrall
walk carefully, walk sure & tall

greet every season with equal joy
be free & love my precious boy

mappa mundi

& where to start
what weight of line

what laboured palette
ground from stone

with hillock or cove
the grip of moss

the moor snow-lipped
or faint with drought

with seas unreined
refracted light

an absence drawn
in silent contours

which trace indicted
which paths unmarked

which muted rock
made cold & sacred

what hieroglyph
to demarcate

the harmonies
of falling leaves

of ice in bloom
the kiss of rain

what weight of line
& where to start

a preface to the fall

& dawn redemptive
refashioning night
into shards of light

we are naked
in the shadows
of lebanese trees

stripped of blame
beyond all censure
we break our fast

plump grapes & figs
their fruit flesh warm
their promise cloys

the snake is just a snake
the devil will wear grey

threnody

rockhampton, qld.

gold & the clip
liquor & grace

sucked down
like plump oysters

by history's
cruel draw

'til everything she
might have been

has disappeared
without a trace

into the light
of some cold day

the tide has ebbed
& all that's left is meat

the watchers

they are with me again
my unpretentious dead

bored with the tedium
of heaven's blank walls

silently they watch me fish
no messages or meaning

no head-fuck revelations
just 12 weightless shadows

perching like cormorants
on the blade of the skere

beneath a blizzard of hungry gulls
the bait-fish run. a fluid thread

of silver knots undone. forsaking
all light for the sanctuary of depth.

the song of remiel

confronted by the glare
of another blank dawn
we stare at this ocean
in muted congregation

anglers & gamblers
bi-lingual romantics
champions of the left
our minds untangling

her strands of cold light
our stance perfected
we salvage grace from
the pains of our labour

hail these angels
of thankless hope

les soixante-huitards

once they dreamed
themselves astride

a barricade of railings
near *porte de paris*

spouting some litany
of hopeful proclamations

daubing crude rainbows
in *rouge* & *noir*

now they have beards
& gall-bladder issues

unhealthy obsessions
with the age of steam

birkenstocks, professorships
the cook-books of diversity

a regular dividend
from the privatised utilities

brigades of children
distant & estranged

whose names are lifted
from an existential genre

all history repackaged
as noble defeat

the solidity of promises
reduced again to air

an epoch of betrayals
exacted in their name

some days i feel
this futile need

for someone else
to shoulder blame

fan ho's vehement lens

here in this town
the dogs are all black

they whine like castrati
at each unfamiliar scent.

the islands bask,
blankly un-empathic,

their poise ungenerous,
their stance averse.

a spite unmasked
in their basalt grins.

the she-oaks flounce,
their branches draped

in swooning flags
set at half-mast.

the bait fish boil,
the turtles dream,

a tern measuring
each fatal swoop.

we languish in the symmetry
of smoke-drenched shadows,

snapping a procession
of bankrupt souls:

the ned kelly beards,
the ill-fitting shorts,

the obesity of privilege,
the obesity of want,

the foxed celtic skin,
rocky's sorrow, sweat & sin,

the miners' thick arms,
the miners' thin wives,

the vacancy of language,
the bulge of their purses,

the hunch of denial,
the shuffle of doubt,

the great white eyes,
the fearful hearts,

the pensioners,
the jettisoned,

the wounded,
& the grinning mad.

they muster
by monuments

to glorious disaster
& the futile dead,

pride in each failure,
guilt in each silence.

inebriate, the larrikin
has pissed in his pants.

a fool, twice so in drink,
he speaks in tongues.

each macho monosyllable
veneered with rum.

a cruciform prostrated
on the bitumen's sweat.

a mother would weep
at seeing his fall.

& here, in this town
the dogs are all black.

the ocean gloats,
pug-nosed & superior;

a smirk on the lip
of each crumbling wave.

like swallows we will leave
when the sun glows cold.

the shortest day

low slung, the remnants
of a fragile sun conspire
to smear the rusted kites;
a conjuring of grace from
the glow of their bellies.
naked & defiant of june's
chill blast, these voiceless
frangipanis rock. all comfort
extracted from the splendour
of their pasts. this season's
trance induced. each bough
reduced to leper's stumps.
they dream themselves
in coats of hopeful bud.

exit

the winter calls time
on a latitude's flirtation.

the thin certainty of departure,
the summoning of futures;

we savour the perfumes
of the last day's sky,

the murmur of the eucalypts'
stertorous locution.

a clutch of spuggies
muster in the eaves,

their chatter self-effacing,
their plumage unfussy;

a meekness to facilitate
our rehabilitation.

dear john

somewhere in the vicinity
of an imagined billabong.

somewhere out country,
but in eye-shot of highlands.

somewhere brick-less,
& blandly mono-cultural.

somewhere vaguely halcyon
with a trace of wood-smoke;

both tranquil & idyllic,
in the clarity of winter.

the illusion of welcome.
a spattering of gums,

a plump wattle in waiting,
a black swan mid-preen.

maybe a sheep,
dourly presbyterian,

maybe a spaniel,
gormless & thirsty,

maybe a remnant
of agrarian toil,

perhaps a glimpse
of imported tweed .

you know the one?
you know the place?

that scene recounted
a thousand times

in vapid, naïve watercolours
by the effete women-folk

of a red-faced squattocracy;
in pristine photo-realistic oils

by the gentlemen tourists
of the royal academy.

& somewhere near
a scene like this,

the nation reclines
rolls out its swag,

emblazoned with eureka's
tattered sack-cloth flag,

unleashes the stench
of a journey's sweat,

of history's dried semen
& the rust of spilled blood;

beds down for the night,
mouths by rote,

(& without particular conviction)
a litany of futile prayers,

finds a hollow in the dirt
for the curve of its hip,

wrestles the discomfort
of its settler's pathology,

carefully compartmentalises
its cornucopia of dread.

& the light on the hill
flickers to extinction,

drowns without ceremony
in a pool of its own wax.

& as simple as that,
as easy as pie,

the vision foreclosed,
the word *egalitarian*

removed from the lexicon
of our jilted ideologies.

any notion of dialectic
lost in the fat rolls

of the obese poor,
in the tear-stained fine-print

of their defaulted mortgages,
in the intricate matrix

of denial & spite
etched in the smirks

of the thin-lipped rich,
in the exquisite apathy

of the middling,
in the sprawling inventory

of their material possessions,
in the blue-lipped silence

of another teenage suicide,
in the bloom of blue bruises

of another battered wife,
the incendiary breath

of a jaundiced alcoholic,
in the shadow of our debt,

the gauntness of the gambler
chasing his own tail,

in drip-fed fears,
in hope denied of means,

enquiry anoxic in the vacuum
of intellectual inertia,

in drought or in flame,
in the face of the other,

in the misinterpreted verses
of someone's holy book,

in the jingoism of failures
& imperial anachronism,

in the glorious technicolour
of a petrol sniffer's dreaming,

in the larrikin grins,
in the churches of athleticism,

in the falsity of memory,
in the bell-jar of constraint,

in the tedious four-stroke refrains
of one dimensional masculinity,

in the shark-eyed hypocrisy
of a palsied democracy,

in the desert of insularity,
in the bankruptcy of morality,

in the silence of the dirt,
in the irritating slowness

of our broadband connectivity,
in the glorious intoxication

of our rampant narcissism,
in the hollow psychologies

of the worried-well
& their unremitting fondness

for collectivised trauma,
in the venal self-interest

of the handmaidens of capital,
in the kookaburra's senseless yakka,

in the insomnia-inducing monotony
of libidinous tree frogs,

in the astounding regenerative
powers of conservatism,

in the white-knuckled grip
of a host of non-specific insecurities,

in the inexcusable lack of craft employed
in the production of the barbecue sausage,

in the entrenched battle-lines
of the history wars,

in the romanticisation of settlement;
with particular reference

to *the man from snowy river*
& every bush-ballad ever written,

in the monarchists' voluminous bleat,
in the perfume of the eucalypt,

in the sweet reek of petrichor,
in the unthinking infatuation with tv chefs

& the ritually commemorative,
in the tumorous mass of our hypochondria

& a continued faith in homeopathy,
in the bleached-out coral of a dying reef,

in the *unavoidable* austerity measures
of our pugilist, neo-con politicos,

in the squalor of manus,
in the stopping of the boats,

in the lame rhetoric of reconciliation,
the insidious dexterity of corporate re-branding,

in the unshiftable stain of patriarchy,
in the burr of a ranter's red raw throat,

in the steadfast march to homogeneity,
in the nuances of a free speech debate,

in the shadow of our hatreds,
in the disempowered majority,

in the solipsistic ephemera
of the legislator poets,

in the impenetrable sophistication
of the doggedly defended,

in the pungency of bat-shit,
in the stultifying absence

of a rigorous critique
of absolutely anything,

in the caul of this dark,
in the curlew's call.

the nation sleeps;
untroubled by the hag

perched on its legs.
it grunts, it snorts,

it twitches like a dreaming dog,
dribbles saliva down its jowls,

unconsciously grips
at the mound of its genitals.

& the light on the hill
flickers to extinction;

drowns without ceremony
in a pool of its own wax.

guerra

carmina mortuorum

'april is the cruellest month, breeding
lilacs out of the dead land, mixing
memory and desires, stirring
dull roots with spring rain.'
ts eliot

i   departure

at albany, replete with pride,
the mother & the pregnant bride
rehearse the detail of their grief.

all innocence dissolved to vain belief
some gentle god will fight beneath
their pristine standard's cotton stars.

administering the last adieu,
the lovers' sacred hearts run through,
each votive mute between their lips.

beyond the range of pomp & streamers,
a quiet rank of larrikins & dreamers
salute the shadow of their youth.

3 score mournful klaxons wail,
euripides & shropshire sail,
an epoch floundering in their wake.

in indian file, they skirt the prow,
dürer's horsemen at their bow,
& silently escape the sound.

ii   danse macabre

they are waltzing matilda
through sheol's cold fire

from every station,
town & shire

within the void
our grief incurs

they glide like angels
toward sauteuse

each footstep grave
as time compels

the lost boys
of the dardanelles

each soul confined
to battle dress

where dread
& longing acquiesce

their faces blunted
by duress

the butcher, the baker
the candle-stick maker

the wages clerk
the undertaker

the shearer, the surgeon
promiscuous & virgin

the squattocrat & hoi polloi
the stockman & the telegram boy

the hewer, the brewer
the preacher, the teacher

the widower & newly wed
the scholar & the dunderhead

the tone deaf tenor
of the broken hill choir

each body cleansed
of blood & mire

they are waltzing matilda
through sheol's cold fire

from every station,
town & shire

each pallid carcass gently bled
to paint the atlas pages red

they dance til endless night gives way
to the bugler's dented reveille

& then they sleep at empire's call
trade breath & dream for bugger all

iii   amara et vanae est…

subservient to rank
& clock the diggers
& their memories
flock to break their fast
with milk & rum.
to ponder the age
they have become.
vale innocence & hail
the larrikin who lost
his smile pursuant
of a crooked mile
of foreign soil. each
dead the day he signed
away his youth to fate.
whose muted lips
commemorate enough.
the rigour of each
tumbling bullet
lodged like nuggets
in his gullet. whose
haunted eyes grew
blind to beauty; each
sacrificed to solemn
duty. each passion dulled,
each vow annulled for
want of faith. each dream
mown down by demons
of insomniac wraith.
the flags are breathless
at half-mast. both patriot
& iconoclast have mustered
as the chaplains pray
beneath the shroud
of reveille. the knowing
mourn; the obligants

suppress a yawn, immune
to grief's infatuation, let
others laud the birth of
nation. another bloated
dignitary is called to lay
a limp bouquet of poppies
wrought from loss & turkish
silk. the honourable member
& their ilk. their faces
wearing tear & frown
as silently the diggers
down their chalices
of poisoned milk.
a host of sleeping angels
bilk the burden of their
sacred care, condemn
their charges to despair.
vale innocence & hail
the mother in a widow's
veil, the father & his
anguished wail,
the johnnies & the poor
mehmets, their legacy
of blunt regrets. the lame,
the mad, their lives
derailed, the ones our
strained compassion
failed. the larrikin who
lost his smile pursuant
of that crooked mile.

legion

i.m. pvt. john parr 1898-1914

the first known casualty was the song of birds;
shocked silent & denied of words. the spiral fizz
of hateful lead arcing like meteors overhead.
& then the meadows, churned to mud, to quagmires
of grief & imperial blood. then faith, then hope;
each hanging like carrion on a gallows' rope.
graceless dead on beds of nettles, loose-draped
in flags of fractured petals. a gouty chaplain's
facile rites condemned him to eternal night.
a marble-mouthed angel dispelling the fear;
as sweet as a blackbird in his deafened ear.
a bitter century unfurled, her dog-eared pages
foxed & curled; a bitter century & still we mourn,
our haunted memes, a muted legion left unborn.

the fighting fifth

'and clay stops many a warrior's mouth'
judith wright

hock-deep, rapacious clarts
reluctantly give up their hold,

our heavy boots death-gripped,
like avid misers' hoarded gold.

& still we march, brave fusiliers,
the order ringing in our ears;

the folly of a slow advance,
commending fate to god & chance.

the spiralling bullet's fatal hiss
bestowing on us its farewell kiss;

our steady rank reduced to meat,
to flesh & blood beneath our feet,

the drills are sewn with splintered bone,
our war is fought, thy will be done.

bait

maryborough, qld.

a million dancing clouds
of pristine smoke
can't cleanse the stain

the dirt, the grass,
the trees imprinted
with its spectre

each seizure, each spasm
each frothing lung
& rictus grin

the koel sings
of poisoned time
& squatter spite

the rigour of hate
the flour laced
the water spiked

each quiet corpse
their fingers stiff
their muted lips

of panic & anoxia
of song-lines drowning
in the gums' slow perfume

of god's blind eyes
each chorus recanting
this sorry business

plantation road

all memory
indentured
to joy & pain.
each journey,
each footfall,
an act of keening.
the grass palms stalk
the blackbirds' ghosts;
each sump, each rise,
each perilous bend
a nom de guerre
transcribed in air.
a feral mango
wilts in alien sun,
its branches writhing
in some torment;
each limb exhausted,
its roots in exile.
at joskeleigh
the camber
of a quiet grave;
bones seek refuge,
a sun-bleached conch,
& muted mizpah.
the longest sleep
to dream of loyalty,
to dream the silence
of a lore's betrayal.

flowers of evil

grey dusk congealed
& gentleness in hiding.
through trembling veils
the truth will mourn itself.
all evil exists in the detail
of its sanction. all hatred
borne of avarice & fear
erupts in blooms quotidian
& sublime. our clamour
for freedom making slaves
of us all. & ask the quiet dead
where terror makes its lair:
in bud dajo, in dresden's flames,
within the breath of my lai's
cordite smog, in hiroshima's
melted time, in beithanoun,
in badajoz & hama or jallianwala
bagh, fort pillow or saltville,
at wounded knee, on the road
to rumaila paved with ill-intent.
a litany replete were ink as free
as idling speech purports to be.

i.m. ibrahim dawawsa

only the minutes
only their distance

to separate survivors
from the dead

a courtyard strewn
with shrapnel petals

a skin of pale dust
as mute as snow

her losses expounded
in each bloody archipelago

only the minutes
only their distance

to demarcate
our hemispheres

to fashion the schism
between hatred & guilt

to furnish these clouds
with absolute burden

their weight aligning
in perfect storms

gaza july 2014

they are joyous & squinting
in the whitewash glare;

feeding pigeons on the roof
of their grandfather's house.

one last gulped breath
to punctuate their laughter.

one graceless shell
to blast them into silence.

their bodies are retrieved;
all trace swilled clean.

except for a clot of feather & blood
cemented to the lip of a fractured drain,

except for the pock of the shrapnel's exuberance,
except for the spaces vacated by prospect.

yukurru

in coniston
the dead still lie
unburied
in an elder's eye

embedded
into bloody lore
collateral
of frontier war

the crows berate
a bell bird chimes
commemorates
the killing times

summary justice
exercised
blunt litanies
of hate reprised

the thirsty soak
still craves for rain
no ritual smoke
can lift the stain

the silence grates
a people's hurt
memorialised
in sanguine dirt

text-book execution

i.m. tunnerminnerwait & maulboyheenner

a crooked mile between
the old eastern watch house
& the cliffs of cape grim
the groaning of gallows
built casual & untrue
the merriment & shame
the weight of their skin
the reverend's lame words
the panic & the drop
the quick heart & taut flax
the mad beak's white logic
the living & the dead
the storm-bird's threnody
let loose on the yarra

ptsd

we shared the prow
but rarely our pasts

i favoured dead-bait
he preferred lures

i knew no more than
his witnessing of war

his preference for the counsel
of fluoxitine & rum

the moon was full
the night he died

a slick on autumn's
first king tide

a boil of pilchards
off the bluff

a gentle blow
in from the east

& naked on the roof
of the veteran's retreat

a paleness contorted
by primal screams

cracking like the static
of scrambled comms

the final call
for mister kurtz

cadenza

cadenza

*'wherever we cry
it is far from home'*
anne michaels

i   the hours

he takes her hand;
a blighted sheaf
of bone & skin
bound loosely
in a callous noose
of some immoral fibre.
an aria of whispers,
comfort in his tender lies;
grace in the weakness
of dawn's pale shadow.

like cats can steal
a baby's breath,
incessant hours
stake claim on yours.

ii notice

despite themselves,
despite this sun's
relentless rays,
they're cold & black,
these summer days.
these cockatoos,
each raucous crest
transformed,
are funeral drays.
each static cloud
above this island
we've made as home,
the smoke & ash
that you'll become.

iii   9 o'clock news

tonight the stars
exert their force

a thousand tonnes
of pressure per lumen

each stacked like hands
on the crown of my head

i dread these calls each
bulletin of hopeless news

her death decanted
into drip-fed dispatches

the moon is weak
a blueness dissolving

like the rhythms
of his voice.

iv mesothelioma

quite a gobful
for untrained
tongues; each
syllable reluctant,
left hanging on
your fragile lips.
a lawless throng
of clustered cells
now mustered from
an epoch's sleep.

i fix on endings:
a bauble of breath,
a flake of heart;
impervious to flame.

v   one last kiss & i'll take my leave

artless & objective,
this photo spits

its difficult truth.
our mam re-cast:

a b-movie zombie
cradling a newborn.

more flesh on a mantis.
her father's strong skull.

her quiet face re-set
in stubborn joy.

a demijohn of morphine
can't quench this love;

the future's weak embers
in the flatness of her eyes.

vi   the hypocrisy of prayer

you will be smiling & in your sleep
mid-way through a *super 8* re-run
of your wedding day (edited of drizzle
& the gnaw of cold) all of us are there;
the living & the dead. all chronology
abandoned. our faces flawless & re-cast.
an endless honour-guard from the church
to the car. grinning like idiots & hurling rice.
& you are resplendent & ripe with hope,
glowing with the aura of a mass-card virgin

no resemblance whatsoever
to a desiccated corpse
strewn in some contortion
in the birkenau clay

vii   anniversary waltz

the music box
is overwound

mimics the silence
of grieving men

stalled mid-bar
a movement lopped

its tin-plate teeth
ground to a halt

for want of tools
chronometry's precision

all remedy evasive
we cannot make good

we cannot make
these hackles sing

viii hall of souls

& the rain will fall
in smoke-blue clouts

fix grey to grey
our sea & sky

rough-shod
but inseparable

we bear the pall
your glass-eyed boys

fragile & cack-handed
there is no weight to it

an ossuary of swan-
bones & familiar skin

the pull of its vacuum
sucking in our cheeks

ix cadenza

dad is reworked
in blanc de chine

his features buckled
like land-bound waves

the sky is gaunt
the crows look on

they skirt our grief
as if contagious

the fire steals
another feast

a whistle of steam
escaping her bones

a single shrill note
hanging in its orbit

x   wake

there is grace
in the small-talk

in the yarned elysium
& the broken smiles

in moments choked
on crumbs of pain

our appetites checked
the plates un-cleared

the gathering dispersed
'til only men are left

their heads in clouds
of whisky & illicit fags

herding their losses
in fields of gaunt silence

xi void

first, the choke
of airless tears

& then a breath
the industry of function

the business of death
the photos re-thumbed

her wardrobe cleared
(but not thrown out)

the heart-break diet
the solace of drink

the lonely walk
the callous void

the callous void
& then the rage

xii vacuum

his days are round
the hours blurred

their futile partition
dissolving into flux

the changing light
the wind & the rain

the song of birds
each arbitrary & vain

a silence communes
with settling dust

his eyes as dulled
as tarnished lead

haunted by the knuckles
of her fleshless spine

xiii   littoral

when warmth returns & gales subside
to pose less mischief. he will scatter
your ashes on the beach at gloucester lodge.
a point equidistant, between the trickle
of maggie's burn & the northernmost
tank-traps; their brutalism fusing with
the hump of a dune. quiet & barefooted,
his trousers at half-mast. his lines rehearsed,
his bon voyage, his last adieu. a brace
of gulls bear curious witness. your dainty
bones reduced to a pigment; now fizzing
like whitewash in a furrow of cold brine.
his question poised: how many slow tides
to wash away the detail of your troubled face?

xiv slick

dawn unleashes
her molten hoard

a lucent slick
assailing land

2 snakebirds wrought
from whitby jet

incise its skin
to break their fast

a boat named *hope*
is coaxed from sleep

she clears her throat
her bilges spit

a shoal of diesel rainbows
spawning in her wake

the aftermath

i   & slow, the dusk

the season ferments;
her fruits fur-draped

lie huddled in the pleats
of a bramble's skirt.

& slow, the dusk will
amble to another death.

the men who grieve
sit down to tea,

dwarfed by the scale
of lonesome rooms.

mechanically they prod
at half-charged plates;

the silence like a callous fact
the moon will shed light on.

ii   fret

dead-slow & anoxic,
an avalanche of muted fog
obliterates the island's smirk.
on grey-scale prows
the cormorants rank
like ghosted tars
stood down from toil
& craving the dram.

we revel in the blur
of wordless calm:
only the palm fronds'
flameless crackle,
the wake of a voyage
dismantled by the shore.

iii   clunk

& grief unravels in
the slowness of dusk.

in the room we do not
open for fear of fear

our histories walk
in ceaseless rings;

slow & unlearning,
contented with their lot,

they drag the heft
of their palsied legs.

a toe-cap scrape,
a clunk, a breath.

a metronome to keep
our time allied to theirs.

iv   cracks

grey stars repent
their hollow pride,

fall from the grip
of sack-cloth sky.

& dawn, impatient,
breaks free of the stalls,

spitting her bridle
of mercury light;

a gloss for the cracks
of a dead-lipped sea.

your absence exceeding
the boundary of measure.

the thinnest breeze & cloud
as pendulous as histories.

v   the phantom dwelling

here, by the ocean
the black mould thrives

relishing the sweat
of these flaking boards

illuminating blankness
with pointillist precision.

& home is just a word
functional & squat

whose ego grows rampant
as ours become fragile

a domicile for prejudice
& festering nostalgia

a house of cards, a roof
above our ghosted heads.

vi skew

only the drone of mowers
& gormless hoons

the graceless anthem
of a crow's bleak cackle

the ocean is honed
to cataract perfection

you are there in the chaos
of these broken waves

a half-smile drowned
in nostalgia's wet kisses

we stop the clock
all memory left skewed

harboured in the flex
of refracted light.

vii summoning

the ocean reflects
the poverty of spring

i turn my back to the land
perch on the prow

of these ancient rocks
a union of monoliths

communing over fault-
lines & our fragile egos

beyond the range
of my longest cast

the bait-fish boil
a summoning of gulls

a swallow makes rest
on the tip of my rod

flare

a season since
& still in her grip

a web of grief,
rapacious loss,

a hold that tightens
with every move:

the unresolved,
the plot extant.

a currawong jigs
on a hot tin roof

this molten light
in vigorous flares

is smeared like spite
on the blades of her hips

the ferryman

in articulo mortis

dad is gripped
by ritual's barbs
he has polished
two old pennies
to place on her eyes

both heads & tails
a mirrored gleam
they warm in his palm
an awkward clink
of guilt & grief

lost to the cadence
of an intravenous drip
[& dubious of silence]
i tell them that *любóвь*
is the russian for love

our hoarded words
are useless now
she has no more to say
her grayscale lips a weld
of thirst & morphine hush

we brace ourselves
our rank of heavy feet
set against the blast
the rattling effervescence
of her drowning lungs

Note: *любóвь* is pronounced lyubov

life lessons from the mermaid café

studious in a tilt-head trance
we watched our mam & dad
spoon-feeding each other
the train-wreck remnants
of a knickerbocker glory

pale fingers entwined
their wedding bands chimed
they leaned into the warmth
of the others' space, still giddy
on the promise of their lips

too soon we are distracted
the urchin spikes of a mk14 sea mine
its threat diminished by candy-stripes
we nag them for coppers for the *rnli*

paradise by the dashboard light

on days like this, the
church of the maudlin
amass to stare at puddles;
drawn to the half-tones
of insignificant car-parks.

bewildered like tourists
alighting their coaches
at hartlepool marina.
a bleak communion
of overdrafts & broken

hearts. they yearn for
meatloaf. the formerly
obese balladeer. the
foodstuff of economy.

fall

the season slips past
& takes you with it.

warmth succumbing
to slow, damp grey.

& dad is reduced;
shrunk to the size

of a songbird's heart.
he drinks to forget

all the things
he has forgotten.

breath indentured
to reckless time;

two spastic hands
left juggling fate.

i wish for him this

let them blow tender
the breezes of spring
free of chill & wild
let them wear promise
in their wayward hair

let dog-rose & the thorny may
capitulate beneath the show
of blossom's pregnant weight
let callous winter take his leave
this grievous curse be null & void

& let there be tumultuous light
unspeaking & empathic
& smeared like honey
on the skin of every dusk

c.v.

the posture of trees, the languages of grass,
the history of clouds, the geometry of flight,

the cadence of dunes, the geography of doubt,
the anatomy of waves, the alchemy of light,

petal & gossamer, the sun & the hoar,
the politics of soil, tenderness & rage,

the rebel & the saint, the flawless ragout,
rapture & pain, a practical array of knots,

the craft of hearing, rudimentary first aid,
the struggle of the hopeful, the art of decay,

the cheek bones of the 3 chord chanteuse,
the dance of flame, the minor keys,

the distance between us. in these i am
qualified; apprenticed & grown expert.

crucible

scorched by loss
we drag the tyne;

a salvage job
reclaiming time.

each saccharin find
a trinket of before,

loose-lipped cobbles
furred with hoar.

an advent market
in seventy-eight

our needs reduced
& less elaborate.

we are pawing over
piles of short-lived tat

i am nagging my mam
for a red-army hat.

she is smiling but deaf
her seduction complete,

lost to the rhythms
of discounted meat.

the river is slack
reflecting on her might

her skin a crucible
of winter light.

archaeology

& bored with the drag
of a summer's slow hours

we took our spades & dug.
lithe prospectors of pre-owned

pasts; harvesting the middens
of the old white rows.

each bulging stratum ripe
raked for bottles & clay pipes,

the mystery of bone
& burnished gelt,

deadweight knuckles
of iron ore set snug

in wombs of feathered ash,
the fractured limbs

of china dolls, their fingers
scuffed, their grip defunct.

today, four decades away,
our mourners' lips as cold

as clay, we'll dig again.
still fluent in the lines

of the riverbank's erosion,
we poke at the shadows

of overhangs, for traces
of redemption. & there,

face down & drowned
in flatulent silt

a hand-blown flagon,
both pristine & flawed,

its skin embellished
with the name of home.

grieve

'black milk of daybreak we drink it at dusk
at noontime and dawn we drink it at night
we drink and we drink'
paul celan

'nothing is as far as truth'
judith wright

nothing more sacred
than grief's black milk

the light & the object
reconciled in shadow

nothing as stubborn
as a blue-lipped kiss

the hollow lyric
of gilded memory

the currency of pasts
a moment defaulted

a cup of ashes
to nourish a rose

an ounce of laughter
to spawn a star

Acknowledgements

Thanks are due to the editors of the following magazines in which many of these poems first appeared: *black light engine room, communion, cordite, idiom 23, otoliths, raum, styluslit, the interpreter's house, the lake, tuck* and *westerly*.

Big thanks too to Tim Thorne, Nathan Curnow, Kristin Hannaford, Peter Shelford & Caroline Beck for their enthusiasm, friendship and constructively critical feedback. Also to Kate Stephenson for giving permission to reproduce *cadenza* (1961) by Ian Stephenson on the front cover. Further information on the artist can be found at: http://www.ianstephenson.net.

Author photo by Simon Veit-Wilson.